BODY CYCLES

BODY CYCLES

MICHAEL ELSOHN ROSS

ILLUSTRATED BY GUSTAV MOORE

THE MILLBROOK PRESS   BROOKFIELD, CONNECTICUT

To Max and Julia—M.R.

For my neighbors, whose helpfulness made this
book possible . . . —G.M.

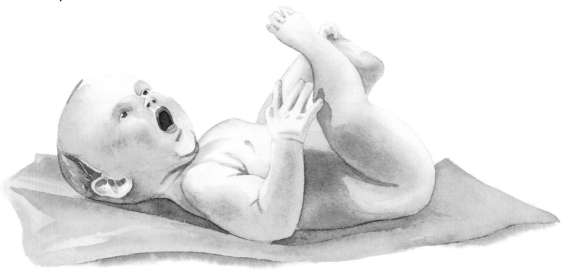

Library of Congress Cataloging-in-Publication Data
Ross, Michael Elsohn, 1952-
Body cycles / by Michael Elsohn Ross; illustrated by Gustav Moore.
p. cm. — (Cycles)
ISBN 0-7613-1816-X (lib. bdg.)
1. Biological rhythms—Juvenile literature. 2. Body, Human—Juvenile literature.
[1. Respiratory system. 2. Skin. 3. Circulatory systems. 4. Cycles.] I. Moore, Gustav ill. II. Title.
QP84.6 .R676 2002   612'.022—dc21   2001030143

Published by The Millbrook Press, Inc.
2 Old New Milford Road
Brookfield, Connecticut 06804
www.millbrookpress.com

A cycle is a pattern that repeats
itself over and over and over.
Your body is always growing.
As you grow, there are many cycles
that happen in your body.

BODY REPAIR CYCLES

As your body grows,
it repairs itself in cycles,
circular patterns that repeat over and over again.
As old parts of your body die, new parts grow to replace them.
Your body changes the food you eat into energy
that helps it regrow new parts.

Each day, like the bark of a tree, you grow new skin,
and old bits of skin are shed.

Each day, like a shedding cat, you grow new hairs, and old hairs drop away.

Each day, like the grass that you mow, your fingernails grow longer,
and when you clip them short, they grow again.

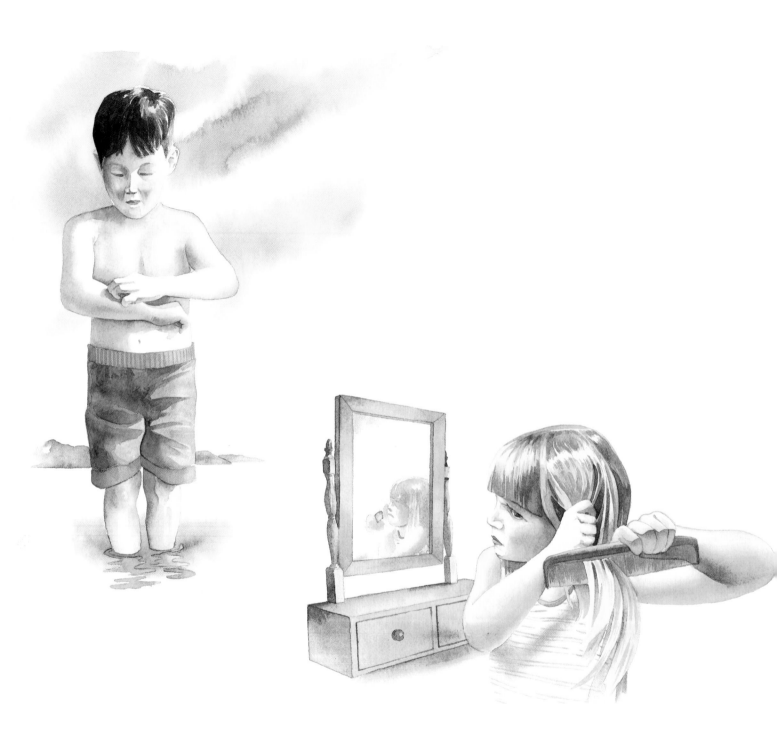

Your body is always growing.
It grows new skin, hair, and fingernails
to replace the old skin, hair, and fingernails that die.

Parts of you grow and die, and new parts grow.

These are cycles that are happening every day.

Food gives your body the energy it needs

to repair itself each day and carry on the cycle of death and regrowth.

BODY REPAIR FACTS

- The human scalp contains an average of about 100,000 hairs, and sheds about 70 to 100 hairs a day.
- The skin is the largest organ of the body.
- Each month, most people's fingernails grow only a fraction of an inch. The longest thumbnail ever recorded measured 4 feet, 8 inches (142 centimeters).

BREATH CYCLES

Inhale.
Exhale.
Inhale.
Exhale.
Over and over again, all day and all night,
you breathe in and breathe out.
Sometimes, on cold days, you can see your breath.

In the air all around you, there is a gas called oxygen.
Your body needs oxygen to survive.
When you breathe in oxygen, your body uses it to help
you get energy from your food.

When your body uses the oxygen to get energy
from your food, you make a new gas called carbon dioxide,
which your body doesn't need. You exhale the carbon dioxide.

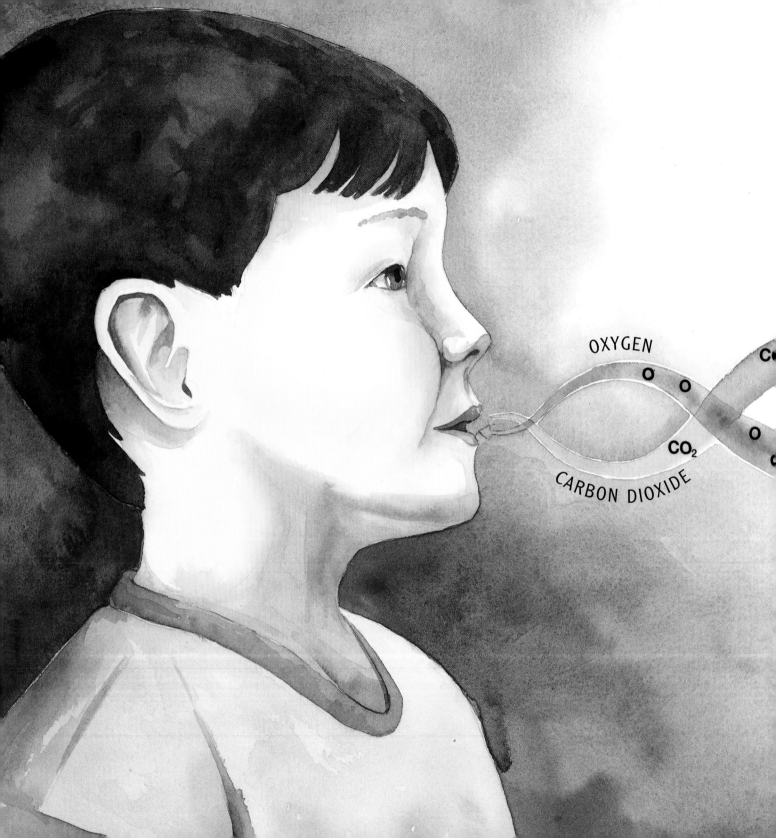

You inhale the air and use the oxygen.
You exhale and get rid of carbon dioxide.
In and out you breathe, over and over and over.
Breathing is a continual cycle of inhaling and exhaling.
It is a cycle that keeps you alive.

CO_2 CO_2

BREATHING FACTS

- When you sneeze, air can shoot out of your nose at more than 100 miles (160 kilometers) an hour!
- People breathe once every two to three seconds—that's about 30,000 to 40,000 times a day.
- The lungs contain about 300 million tiny air sacs, called alveoli. If all these sacs were flattened out, they would cover an area of as much as 1,000 square feet (93 square meters).

THE BLOOD CYCLE

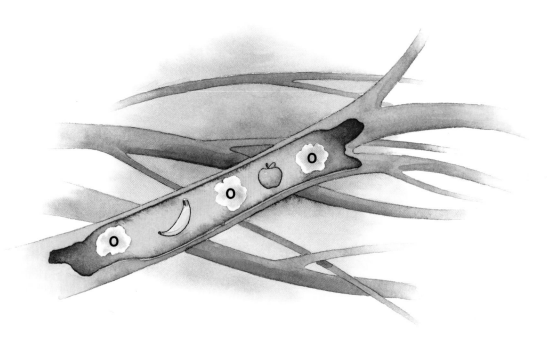

Thump,

Thump,

Thump.

Feel your heart beat.

It is pumping blood throughout your body.

It pumps blood that carries oxygen from your lungs and food energy from your stomach and intestines to all the cells that make up your body.

Your blood picks up oxygen
in your lungs when you inhale.

Your blood picks up food energy in your stomach and intestines when you eat.

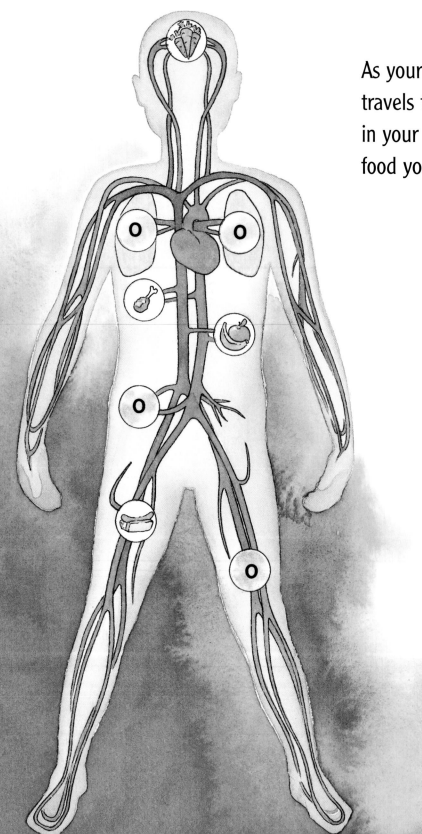

As your heart pumps, the blood travels through arteries to all the cells in your body, delivering the oxygen and food your cells need.

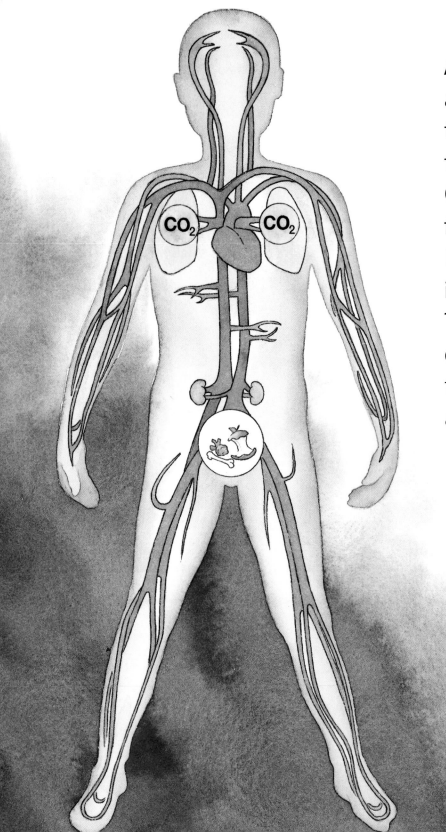

After the blood has delivered oxygen
and food to your cells,
the heart pumps the blood back to
the lungs through your veins.
On its way it leaves behind
food waste in your kidneys.
It leaves behind carbon dioxide
in your lungs.
Then your blood picks up fresh
oxygen and new food energy in
the lungs and starts the cycle
all over again.

Your blood flows around your body in a cycle.
It travels from your heart through your arteries
to every part of your body.
Then it travels back to your heart again through your veins.
This is called circulation. Circulation has part of the word "circle" in it.
That is because the blood goes around and around in your body in a
circle-like cycle that nourishes every cell in your body.

CIRCULATION FACTS

- There are thousands of miles of veins and arteries in your body, enough, in fact, to wrap twice around the world and still have some left over.
- Your blood flows from your heart, through your arteries to every part of your body and back again more than 1,000 times a day.
- A three-year-old child has about a quart (almost a liter) of blood in circulation. An adult, depending on weight, will have about five times that amount.

A cycle is any pattern that repeats itself
over and over and over.
Each time your body repairs itself,
each time you breathe,
each time your heart beats,
parts of your body travel in circular patterns called cycles.

ABOUT THE AUTHOR AND ARTIST

Michael Elsohn Ross lives at the entrance of Yosemite National Park, California, on a bluff overlooking the wild Merced River. For more than 25 years Michael has been teaching Yosemite visitors about the plants, animals, and geology of the park. He leads classes and backpack trips for the Yosemite Association and is the educational director of Yosemite Guides. His work in the park and as a science educator have inspired him to write more than 30 books for young people, including **Become a Bird and Fly**, and **Earth Cycles** and **Life Cycles**, the first two volumes in the Cycles series. Many of his books have been named to the Outstanding Science Trade Books for Children list by the National Science Teachers Association/Children's Book Council.

Growing up in rural Maine, Gustav Moore had boyhood adventures in the woods and fields of his family's farm that gave him a deep appreciation and love of the natural world. His colorful and detailed watercolor paintings reflect this beauty and wonder of nature. He has illustrated four earlier books for children: **Stonewall Secrets**, which was recognized as a 1998 Notable Children's Book by Smithsonian, **Everybody's Somebody's Lunch**, **Earth Cycles**, and **Life Cycles**. Gustav Moore works and lives in Maine, where he still wanders the open pastures of the family farm, finding inspiration in the cycles of nature.